WRITINGS ON WRITING

26,

p 11,140

Writings
on
Writing

by

May Sarton

Puckerbrush Press, Orono, Maine

ACKNOWLEDGEMENTS

Grateful acknowledgement is made for permission to reprint these articles:

"The School of Babylon" is reprinted from the collection of essays, *A Celebration of Poets,* edited by Don Cameron Allen and published by The Johns Hopkins University Press. Copyright © 1959, 1962, 1967, by The Johns Hopkins Press, Baltimore, Md. 21218.

"The Writing of a Poem" and "The Design of a Novel" were addresses delivered at Scripps College and published, in pamphlet form, by Scripps College, Claremont, California. Copyright © 1957 and 1963, respectively, by May Sarton.

"Revision as Creation: The Growth of a Poem" is reprinted from the CEA *Critic,* June, 1967. Copyright © 1967, by the College English Association.

"On Growth and Change" is reprinted by permission from *The Christian Science Monitor.* Copyright © 1966, by The Christian Science Publishing Society. All rights reserved.

First Printing December, 1980
Second Printing February, 1981
Third Printing November, 1981
Fourth Printing April, 1982
Fifth Printing February, 1983
Sixth Printing January, 1984
Revised Edition September, 1986
Eighth Printing February, 1988
Ninth Printing January, 1990
Tenth Printing October, 1992

ISBN 0-913006-20-3

Printed in the United States of America
by Howland's Printing Company, Old Town, Maine
Bound by University of Maine Press

Contents

The School of Babylon

This is the School of Babylon
And at its hands we learn
To walk into the furnaces
And whistle as we burn.
                                    Thomas Blackburn

I MUST WARN YOU at once that I am not a critic, except of my own work, but perhaps I should not offer this fact as an apology for surely the great poet-critics of our time —Yeats, Valery, Eliot—have used what has been sometimes taken as dispassionate criticism of others as a means of orienting themselves and of grounding their own work in an aesthetic. Perhaps criticism from poets is always self-criticism.

I should like to reconsider and shape once more some tentative answers to questions I have been asking myself for many, many years, questions about tension and equilibrium within the writing of poetry and within the poet's life.

5

Eugen Herrigel in a small but explosive book, *Zen in the Art of Archery*, speaks of the aim of the Zen masters as not "the ability of the sportsman, which can be controlled, more or less, by bodily exercises, but an ability whose origin is to be sought in spiritual exercises and whose aim consists in hitting a spiritual goal, so that fundamentally the marksman aims at himself and may even succeed in hitting himself." So let me draw my bow and point the arrow inward . . .

I have an idea that somewhere in his forties the poet reaches a turning point, at which he either becomes a more public or a more private person, that he has a choice, and on that choice depends the kind of work he will produce, as well as the kind of life he will live. In the dialogue between the world and himself, he fights to preserve the innocence and the intensity without which art cannot exist. And it is just when he is in his forties that the pressures to lecture, to review other men's books, and to be a public person begin to assert themselves. My theme is tension in equilibrium, that dangerous tension, that perilous equilibrium which exist in every great poem, and in the life of every poet; and I have just touched on one of the permanent tensions, that between the public and the private person, the poet who lectures and the poet who writes the poems: they are opposite poles. Each of us seeks out his own solution to this never-solved problem. But I suspect, nevertheless, that the tension between the public and private self is not an unfruitful one. One of the fascinations of Yeats' growth is that his assaults on the world, as a founder of the Abbey Theatre, and later as a senator, helped him to forge his style. Without the fierce tension between what he called "The Mask and the Self," would he have hammered out the iron of his later style? Who knows?

Tension . . . my Webster defines it in several ways. Here are three which I can appropriate: 1) A strained condition of relations, as between nations. 2) A device to produce a desired tension or pull, as in a loom. 3) *Elec.*: The quality in consequence of which an electric charge tends to discharge itself.

As I pondered these provocative definitions, I jotted down some of the tensions I experience in the process of writing a poem, tensions which discharge a load of experience in a most beneficent and exciting way when the piece of weaving on the loom turns out to be a real poem:

1) The tension between past and present,
2) between idea and image,
3) between music and meaning,
4) between particular and universal,
5) between creator and critic,
6) between silence and words.

Parallel with them are the tensions within daily life:

1) between the living and the dead,
2) between the public and the private person,
3) between art and life.

Once I had noted down these apparently organized but actually haphazard ideas, I took refuge at once in the equilibrium and organization of a poem, Thomas Blackburn's "The School of Babylon," from which I have borrowed the title of this essay. (The relief it was to rest in this "momentary stay against confusion"!) I might tell you that the epigraph of Blackburn's poem is from Daniel, "Men loose walking in the midst of fire" (3:25). This is the second and final stanza:

> Although a wine-glass or a cup
> Can hold as little of the sea
> As you and I of our own selves,
> Pin-pointed by mortality,
> We still, that something of the whole,

May quicken in the finite part,
Must labour for a deeper breath
And greater tension of the heart.
Out of their windy distances
The further energies draw near
And kindling in our tongues and hands
Increase the glory and the fear.
But still as the unspoken word
Swings slowly downward into speech
And in becoming us reveals
Another word beyond our reach,
We praise the School of Babylon,
For where else could we learn
To walk into the furnaces
And whistle as we burn?

Of course, one of the springs of poetry is our strained relations with our own immediate past, the warring nations within the self; then the poem itself becomes a device by means of which this electric charge discharges itself. And one of the springs of poetry is joy—joy and grief as opposed to happiness and depression; the difference in *intensity* between the former and the latter is my point. In a formal sense, each poem also discharges and balances the tension between the whole past of poetic invention and itself; each new poem is partly propelled by the formal energies of all the poems that have preceded it in the history of literature. Those poets who wish to affirm their freedom from the past by pretending that all old forms are dead, deny themselves this fruitful tension. Their poems are intended to be wholly "present," but we experience the present as a kind of equilibrium between past and future, and there is only tension, no balance between present and future. Such poems, like the children of *Brave New World*, are test-tube poems. I think that the answer may be in the distance in time between the points of tension: we have to move back more than one generation to find the fruitful polarity. Valery makes this clear in his unexpected praise of Victor Hugo (the poet's Hugo as against the public's Hugo) for going back to the then unfashionable sixteenth-century French poets for some of his forms. So Hugo remains a source in a way that Vigny, de Musset, Lamartine do not.

"The poetic player," as Valery puts it in another context, "can choose his game: some prefer roulette, others chess." If you are a chess player, what you are looking for is a new opening, a new device by which you may win within the old rules; a means of taking your opponent by surprise. The dynamics of form have to do with our intimate relation with the past, and our natural instinct for what we can use for a particular poem, the form that can best become a vehicle for its electric current, the tension between the whole rich past and this poem *now*. Like a pregnant woman who must suddenly have strawberries, I once found myself going back to Herbert for the form of a poem which created an equilibrium for me (in this case a permanent one) out of the excruciating tensions set up by my mother's death from cancer. The poem itself I could only write four years later; I could write it partly because I had found in George Herbert a viable structure.

Sometimes the polarity expresses itself, not through metrics, but by means of an echo. Eliot has often used this device, in the earlier poems for purposes of irony, in the later ones as a way of condensing time. How effective it can be, Yeats proved in "A Bronze Head," when suddenly he allows Herbert and the particular reverberations Herbert brings with him to act as catharsis for his revaluation of Maud Gonne. I need not remind you of the climax of Herbert's "The Collar":

> But as I rav'd and grew more fierce and wilde
> At every word,
> Me thought I heard one calling, *Child!*
> And I reply'd, *My Lord.*

Here is the third stanza of "A Bronze Head":

> But even at the starting-post, all sleek and new,
> I saw the wildness in her and I thought
> A vision of terror that it must live through
> Had shattered her soul. Propinquity had brought
> Imagination to that pitch where it casts out
> All that is not itself: I had grown wild
> And wandered murmuring everywhere, 'My child, my child!'

And let us not forget that, as Valery says, "Everyone knows that to aim at not following or imitating someone is still in some way to imitate him. The mirror reverses images." The poet cannot escape from the tension between past and present even when the tension is expressed by total rejection of the past.

He cannot do so any more than any one of us can escape from our individual past, for to do so is to murder a part of ourselves. The tension between the living and the dead, especially perhaps that between oneself and one's parents, after their death, may become especially powerful in middle age. Yeats' father and grandfather are always there back of the poems, and so too with Edwin Muir. I must regard my whole life as an attempt to bring into focus and so be able fully to use the rich gifts I was given by a scholar father and an artist mother, each strong in his own right. I do not summon them, but they are there, pivotal tensions. Everything must be tested and questioned against their innocence, their passion, and my whole life a precarious balance between their two kinds of genius.

Let us return to poetry itself and the writing of poems. At once I find myself rebelling against the act of criticism because it must, if it is to explain anything at all, make an indivisible act divisible and partial. In fact, it is possible that we recognize the birth of a true poem as distinct from what Louise Bogan calls "imitation poems" by this very state, a state in which a series of complexes exist *together*, and find their way to equilibrium without ever having been separated out into distinct functions or threads. Idea and image, music and meaning, creation and criticism, the particular and the universal, silence and utterance—when we are ready to write a poem, all these separate modes work together at the same time. "Poetry," as Valery puts it, "must extend over the whole being; it stimulates the muscular organization by its rhythms, it frees or unleashes the verbal faculties, ennobling their whole action, it regulates our depths, for poetry aims to arouse or reproduce the unity and harmony of the living person, an extraordinary unity that shows itself when a man is possessed by an intense feeling that leaves none of his powers disengaged." Unfortunately the act of criticism imposes the necessity to disengage certain powers, and is therefore always in some sense, false.

A true poem does not begin with a feeling, however compelling, and of course we feel a great many things that never become poems. A poem emerges when a tension that *has been* something experienced, felt, seen, suddenly *releases* a kind of anxious stirring about of words and images; at this moment there is a mysterious shift of energy; the energy that was absorbed in experience itself, now becomes an energy of an entirely different kind, and all that matters is to solve the sort of puzzle, the sort of maze in which certain phrases, and a certain rhythm lie around like counters in a game of Scrabble. So a great grief may turn into a certain kind of imaginative energy and lift the sufferer right out of himself into the joys of creation.

Let me give you a ludicrous example which will serve as well as any to give you some idea as to how the process works. Some years ago I was given a magnificent Teddy bear as a Valentine and he has become one of the Lares, sits on a big desk in the little parlor and emits a muted bellow when you pick him up. One day I seemed to hear him singing a little song, a rhyme, and, once in my head, I could not get it out for a whole day. It goes

Only, only,
lonely, lonely,
moanly, moanly,
groanly, groanly.

True poems may make their appearance in just the way
this rhyme did, and take over the day, interrupt whatever
we may be doing, insist on making themselves heard,
willy-nilly. For us, who are not Teddy bears, the music
may be more subtle, though it may not (you remember
Edith Sitwell's "Daisy and Lily, lazy and silly," no
doubt?). In a true poem, this "musical stir" as Maritain
calls it, this tension of a phrase asking to be musically
resolved, is always accompanied by an image. The rhyme
of the bear is not a poem for many reasons, and one is
that the bear himself does not appear. If the bear-song
could have incorporated bear himself, it might have
become one. Everything in the psyche takes place for a
reason. Why did something in me identify itself with the
Teddy bear? No doubt I too was feeling lonely and moanly. If this state had been about to be translated into a
poem, I would have had to enter the maze of bear, the
puzzle of bear, and find my way out of it, or rather *into* its
center and heart. And I might have sat down to ask myself
some questions.

Did the bear begin to sing for me because he suggests
innocence, childhood, and also the whole unconscious
animal world, the sensual world, of which at that time I
felt deprived? And is the sensual world always there when
we feel wholly ourselves? So that to be deprived of our
animal self is in some way to be deprived also of its
polarity, the angel self? The bear seems also to be con-
solation—he sings a lonely song because I feel lonely,
and I am comforted by this image of childhood. Why is
an image of childhood consoling to an adult?

But while I am asking myself these questions, the
music the bear is chanting runs along all the time under-
neath, emerging now and then into an actual phrase,

imposing upon me the metrical form the poem will take. And a high tension, a delightful inner humming is set up between the apparently innocuous rhyme, the image back of it, and my own response, both conscious and unconscious, to what is going on in my head.

There are points at which the arts, especially those of painting and poetry, bisect each other. Painters, too, think their way through, by means of images lifted out by a present shock of emotion, and polarizing the whole past. I want to steal here a fairly long excerpt from Ben Shahn's book *The Shape of Content.* He is analyzing the sources of a painting of his called "Allegory." The immediate seminal image was that of a fire in Chicago in which a man had lost his four children.

> It seemed to me that the implications of this event transcended the immediate story; there was a universality about man's dread of fire, and his sufferings from fire. There was a universality in the pity which such disaster invokes. Even racial injustice, which had played its part in this event, had its overtones. . . .
>
> I now began to devise symbols of an almost abstract nature, to work in terms of such symbols. Then I rejected that approach too. For in the abstracting of an idea one may lose the very intimate humanity of it, and this deep and common tragedy was above all things human. I returned then to the small family contacts, to the familiar experiences of all of us, to the furniture, the clothes, the look of ordinary people, and on that level made my bid for universality and for the compassion that I hoped and believed the narrative would arouse.
>
> Of all the symbols which I had begun or sought to develop, I retained only one in my illustrations—a highly formalized wreath of flames with which I crowned the plain shape of the house which had burned. . . .
>
> The narrative of the fire had roused in me a chain of personal memories. There were two great fires in my own childhood, one only colorful, the other disastrous and unforgettable. Of the first, I remember only that the little Russian village in which my grandfather lived burned, and I was there. I remember the excitement, the flames breaking out everywhere, the lines of men passing buckets to and from the river which ran through the town, the mad-woman who had escaped from someone's house during the

confusion, and whose face I saw, dead-white in all the reflected color.

The other fire left its mark upon me and all my family, and left its scars on my father's hands and face, for he had clambered up a drain-pipe and taken each of my brothers and sisters and me out of the house one by one, burning himself painfully in the process. Meanwhile our house and all our belongings were consumed, and my parents stricken beyond their power to recover.

Among my discarded symbols pertaining to the Hickman story there were a number of heads and bodies of beasts, besides several Harpies, Furies, and other symbolic semi-classical shapes and figures. Of one of these, a lion-like head, but still not a lion, I made many drawings, each drawing approaching more nearly some inner figure of primitive terror which I was seeking to capture. I was beginning to become most familiar with this beast-head. It was, you might say, under control. . . .

When at last I turned the lion-like beast into a painting, I felt able to imbue it with everything that I had ever felt about a fire. I incorporated the highly formalized flames from the Hickman story as a wreath about its head, and under its body I placed the four child figures which, to me, hold the sense of all the helpless and innocent.

The image that I sought to create was not one of *a* disaster; that somehow does not interest me. I wanted instead to create the emotional tone that surrounds disaster; you might call it inner disaster.

When I read these pages, I recognized the analogy with a poet's images and how he unearths them. For here, too, we may sometimes begin with an actual scene, witnessed, but it will only become material for poetry if it is able to magnetize to itself a part of the inner world as well, if it reverberates. There is some truth, I think, in the criticism of the poets called "academic" (I fear I am one of them!) for being overconcerned with the decorative aspects of language. A poem does not move us deeply, I believe, unless the central image is capable of stirring us below the level of consciousness, is, in fact, an archetype. For the metaphor holds the explosive power of the poem. This explosion may take place on the surface of the mind, in which case it gives a moment's pleasure, or it may take place in the mysterious inner recesses of being, in which case the poem may well do what Rilke asks of art at the end of his sonnet on the "Archaic Torso of Apollo":

> Here there is nothing that does not see you:
> You must change your life.

The most viable metaphor contains the greatest possible number of tensions and at the same time releases them. And we are changed by it not because we have been told about something, but because a whole series of inner actions have been set in motion by it and at the same time to some extent resolved. Something has been changed at the center of consciousness, forever.

The surface image is a temptation to every poet; for if he is a poet at all, he is apt to think in images and every abstract idea comes to him immediately translated into a concrete exemplar. But every time he writes a real poem, he will find himself polarized in a tension so complex and painful that it forces him to deepen and explore below the surface.

Tension between idea and image has to do with the depth and complexity of the image; if it is an inspired image, i. e., one that comes from deep enough below the surface, it may very probably change the original idea, for the image is all the time pointing the way to what we really mean, and not what we thought we meant. In this sense the image is ethical. As Bachelard, the French psychologist who has devoted himself to examining metaphor, says: "we are here at a center where ideas dream and where images think."

"The Combat" by Edwin Muir throws us a naked metaphor so powerful that I have never recovered from my first reading of it, and to re-read it is merely to resume aloud, the uninterrupted reverberations that it set up.

> It was not meant for human eyes,
> That combat on the shabby patch

Of clods and trampled turf that lies
Somewhere beneath the sodden skies
For eye of toad or adder to catch.

And having seen it I accuse
The crested animal in his pride,
Arrayed in all the royal hues
Which hide the claws he well can use
To tear the heart out of the side.

Body of leopard, eagle's head
And whetted beak, and lion's mane,
And frost-grey hedge of feathers spread
Behind—he seemed of all things bred.
I shall not see his like again.

As for his enemy, there came in
A soft round beast as brown as clay;
All rent and patched his wretched skin;
A battered bag he might have been,
Some old used thing to throw away.

Yet he awaited face to face
The furious beast and the swift attack.
Soon over and done. That was no place
Or time for chivalry or for grace.
The fury had him on his back.

And two small paws like hands flew out
To right and left as the trees stood by.
One would have said beyond a doubt
This was the very end of the bout,
But that the creature would not die.

For ere the death-stroke he was gone,
Writhed, whirled, huddled into his den,
Safe somehow there. The fight was done,
And he had lost who had all but won.
But oh his deadly fury then.

A while the place lay blank, forlorn,
Drowsing as in relief from pain.
The cricket chirped, the grating thorn

Stirred, and a little sound was born.
The champions took their posts again.

And all began. The stealthy paw
Slashed out and in. Could nothing save
These rags and tatters from the claw?
Nothing. And yet I never saw
A beast so helpless and so brave.

And now, while the trees stand watching, still
The unequal battle rages there.
The killing beast that cannot kill
Swells and swells in his fury till
You'd almost think it was despair.

There, I hope you will agree, is an image in poetry that can be set beside Ben Shahn's lion-head of fire.

Just as we "must labour for a deeper breath and greater tension of the heart" when we come to use or discard the metaphors that pass through the waking mind when a poem is in process, so we must labour too, to deepen, and even sometimes roughen, the too facile music that floats about on the surface of consciousness. Yeats spent a lifetime working toward the tone, the rhythm, the tune that would express the rigor and complexity of what he had to say as he moved away from the superficial singing of the Lake Isle toward the resinous speech of the Last Poems. In a letter of 1916, he is already worrying this problem: "I separate the rhythmical and the abstract. They are brothers, but one is Abel and one is Cain. In poetry they are not confused for we know that poetry is rhythm, but in music-hall verses we find an abstract cadence, which is vulgar, because it is apart from imitation. This cadence is a mechanism, it never suggests a voice shaken with joy or sorrow as poetical rhythm does. It is but the noise of a machine and not the coming and going of the breath."*

---

*The Letters of W. B. Yeats, Macmillan and Company, New York, 1955.

Poetry finds its perilous equilibrium somewhere between music and speech, and each poet as he comes along
has to breathe his own breath, find his own intervals
that will make it "sound right" for him. How various the
solutions may be can be apprehended if we juxtapose
Robert Frost and Paul Valery! One reason I have found
myself going back to Herbert is to try to catch his intervals, the swing of his pendulum between music and
meaning, between music and speech. . . ; we are not
floated down the poem like paper boats; we are absorbed into it by strange little pauses and irregularities
of breathing, as if indeed a voice were speaking aloud
to us now:

> Ah, my deare angrie Lord,
> Since thou dost love, yet strike;
> Cast down, yet help afford;
> Sure I will do the like.
>
> I will complain, yet praise;
> I will bewail, approve:
> And all my soure-sweet dayes
> I will lament, and love.

Even when he uses this simplest of all forms, you see,
the cadence is highly individual, his own voice.

Once again—it is, after all, my theme—what becomes
clear is that facility (lack of tension) is the enemy of
poetry. The very poverty of rhyme in the English language gives us an advantage, I sometimes think, over
the French poet, crowded in, as by a flock of pigeons, by
the hundreds of rhyming words. Rhyme in English is a
hard master. The obstacles that it raises in the current of
our thought slow us down, make us think, and of course
also sometimes (there is a saving grace!) bring us the
lucky chance that may enrich meaning in unexpected
ways.

> I could give all to Time except—except
> What I myself have held.

says Mr. Frost. Might one not speak in somewhat the same terms of the struggle within the writing of each poem? A great deal has to be given up, so that when we come to the end, we do say, "And what I would not part with, I have kept." We have come through some real dangers and taken some real risks. The music, the images, and the propulsive idea, all these make intricate and sometimes apparently opposite demands. From the tensions between them, when they arrive at an equilibrium, poised on all the dangers, like a bird in the air, the poem soars. As Henry Adams says at the end of *Mont St. Michel and Chartres,* "The equilibrium is visibly delicate beyond the line of safety; danger lurks in every stone."

I fear I have been rather solemn about what the French troubadours knew as the "gai scavoir." But I hope it goes without saying that, just as the joy of playing tennis for the player is the mastery of the continual stress of the game, and if it were easier to play, it would not be half as much fun, so the poet of course is never happier, nor more wholly himself, than when he is engaged in the play of writing a poem, in making the puzzle "come out right." And the longer he can tease it along, the happier he is, if he is a poet like Valery. Of course there is the final danger of crossing the intangible frontier beyond which a poem is damaged by more manipulation. . . ; it may suddenly go dead like the mouse which the cat has played with. When is a poem finished?

The answer is, I think, when all the tensions it has posited are perfectly equilibrated, when the change of a single syllable would so affect the structure that the poem would fall like a house of cards under the shift. But Valery's answer to when a poem is finished would be, "never." Valery was that rarest of poets—one for whom the ultimate release was in the artifice itself (he did not *want* to finish), as against Yeats for whom the release was in equilibrating tensions *back* of the poem *by means* of it. Yeats could say, "They and their sort alone earn

contemplation, for it is only when the intellect has
wrought the whole of life to drama, to crisis, that we may
live for contemplation and yet keep our intensity."
Valery could say, "My poem 'Le Cimetiere Marin' began
in me by a rhythm, that of a French line . . . of ten sylla-
bles, divided into four and six. I had as yet no idea with
which to fill this form. Gradually a few hovering words
settled in it, little by little determining the subject. . . ."
I need not remind you, I am sure, that this turned into
one of the few great metaphysical poems written in our
time. It is clear that we do not exactly choose our poems;
our poems choose us.

Poems may never be finished if one is Valery, but
essays must come to an end. It was my intention when I
began to think about *The School of Babylon* to avoid
using any poem of my own as illustration. But it now
seems to me that the analysis of someone else's poem
could be an act of hubris. For who am I to describe the
process by which any of them came into being? I can
only speak with authority about process in relation to
my own work.

Probably Thomas Blackburn's poem moves me as it
does because it articulates almost every element that goes
into the writing of poetry and the poet's life as I see them.
The refrain of the first stanza, the one I did not quote
goes:

> This is the School of Babylon
> And at its hands we learn
> To walk into the furnaces
> And whistle as we burn.

Here we find Yeats' vision and Valery's fused. We must
be "men loose walking in the midst of fire," and men or
women who find it possible to whistle as they burn.
The writing of poetry is the whistling. But if we did not
dare walk into the furnaces, there would be no occasion
for whistling. Whistling in the dark is another matter!

We go to school to a complex, demanding art so that we may learn a device for discharging tensions and apprehensions which we might not otherwise have strength to bear, and which as it is, become simply transposable *energy*. So grief itself is transposed into a curious joy.

I shall tell of a poem of mine called "Lifting Stone." The image came to me through a painting by Katharine Sturgis, a semiabstract water color of a piece of granite being lifted out of a quarry. I saw the painting first more than ten years ago, but could not afford to buy it. Still, it haunted me. And when it reappeared, in a show, still unsold, years after my first meeting with it, I felt this was a sign. I had better buy it and live with it and understand *why* I was haunted.

The image was evidently one of those complex ones which had something to reveal if I could explore it down deep enough, explore it by making a poem out of it. Quarries give us to dream. I sensed slowly that one of the reasons why is the fact that we dig down deep into the earth to bring up the stones that will eventually soar in the cathedrals—as we dig down to the subconscious matrix to bring up the images that fertilize the imagination. No height without depth.

But there was another element in the painting, the equilibrium of the pulley itself, lifting this immense stone pillar on a steel thread, as if the stone were a mere feather. Here tension could be seen equilibrated in the most delicate possible way. Thirdly, in Katharine Sturgis' painting, the whole composition centered in the abstract figure of a man, standing way down deep inside, directing the operation. I had at the time been reading Herrigel. Let us go back to him for a moment now. Herrigel worked for five years with a Zen master in Japan before he even began to learn the self-abstraction and the technical skill to understand the art of the archer. Sometime in the fifth year he tells us,

One day the Master cried out the moment my shot was loosed: "It is there! Bow down to the goal!" Later, when I glanced towards the target—unfortunately I couldn't help myself—I saw that the arrow had only grazed the edge. "That was a right shot," said the Master decisively, "and so it must begin. But enough for today, otherwise you will take special pains with the next shot, and spoil the good beginning. . . ."

During those weeks and months I passed through the hardest schooling of my life, and though the discipline was not always easy for me to accept, I gradually came to see how much I was indebted to it. It destroyed the last traces of any preoccupation with myself and the fluctuations of my mood. "Do you now understand," the Master asked me one day after a particularly good shot, "what I mean by 'It shoots,' 'It hits'?"

"I'm afraid I don't understand anything more at all," I answered, "even the simplest things have got into a muddle. Is it 'I' who draws the bow, or is it the bow that draws me into the state of highest tension? Do 'I' hit the goal, or does the goal hit me? Is 'It' spiritual when seen with the eyes of the body, and corporeal when seen by the eyes of the spirit—or both or neiher? Bow, arrow, goal and ego, all melt into one another, so that I can no longer separate them. And even the need to separate has gone. For as soon as I take the bow and shoot, everything becomes clear and straightforward and ridiculously simple. . . ."

"Now at last," the Master broke in, "the bowstring has cut right through you."

What held me here, as it did in Katharine Sturgis' painting, was once more that at the point of highest tension, lies also the point of supreme release. In the end what is most difficult becomes most easy, what was heaviest to lift becomes light as air . . . and this happens, of course, when we are not thinking of ourselves at all, but have become instruments of an art or craft. At such a time it may be possible for a master like Frost in the art of poetry to sit down after a long night's work on something else and set down "Stopping by Woods on a Snowy Evening," without a pause, as a Japanese painter in one stroke paints a piece of bamboo and it is "right."

Lifting Stone

This is an ancient scene: we stand and stare
As hills are excavated and then lifted;
Swung on the cable's perpendicular,
The load is pivotal to earth and air,
A feather-balance, and so delicate
The stone floats up as if it had no weight.

Below, a solitary figure stands
To gentle the long bundle from its bed;
Athens and Troy are leaning from his hands;
The Roman arch, then perilous Chartres ascends
Out of the empty spacious world where he
Nudges rich burdens toward history.

Who with his own machineries of skill
Has not dreamed often of this very place?
Painter and poet lift the buried hill
To build a pyramid or clean bright wall,
And the great spires that sleep in this quarry
Are excavated toward the clouds they marry.

What soars is always buried deep for ages,
Gently explored in the hill's dark mind,
Prized, hewn in slow thoughtful stages,
Then floated on these airy equipages,
Watched by a figure standing there alone
Whose work, humble and hard, is lifting stone.

The Design of a Novel

I AM OFTEN TROUBLED by the enormity of having under-
taken to explore two crafts instead of one, two difficult
crafts, each of which could command a lifetime's imagination and effort. But there are some things the novel can
do which poetry cannot do; lyric poetry is concerned
chiefly with the moment's intense vision, the vision of
one person; the novel is concerned with the inter-relation
of several—and sometimes many—psyches and their
impact on each other. It is concerned with growth. A
novel requires a long breath, *un long souffle* as the
French would say. It can, to some extent, be planned
ahead over a considerable period of time. One can say,
"I am going to write a novel next year," but one cannot
say, "I am going to write a poem next year." Intellect
and will do not control poetry to the same extent. Nevertheless we are always in deep mysterious waters when-

ever we try to analyse a creative process. Let me lean for a moment on E. M. Forster's arm. When asked by one of the *Paris Review* interviewers, "How aware are you of your own technical competence?" Forster answered, "People will not realize how little conscious one is of these things; how one flounders about. They want us to be so much better informed than we are. If critics could only have a course in writers *not* thinking things out—a course of lectures. . . ."

Where does the idea for a novel come from? What kind of idea is it? And how do you recognize that it is a fertile one? It may be that if it looks like "a great idea" it will in the end turn into a mediocre novel. Many a schema for an American *War and Peace* has finally been thrown in the wastebasket. The fruitful idea may well spring from something seen out of the corner of an eye, perhaps a place, perhaps a person, perhaps a situation suggested by an overheard remark—the seed may lie dormant for a long time, but little by little it magnetizes the imagination. It begins to *haunt*. I might add that the seed of an idea for a novel seems to take a considerable time to germinate. What does "haunting" imply in this context? That the idea has slipped down into the layers of the unconscious where it is fertilized by some unexplored but actual experience of one's own which "wants out"? One is not usually haunted by something as clear as daylight. My own feeling is that the only possible reason for engaging in the hard labor of writing a novel, is that one is bothered by something one needs to understand, and can come to understand only through the characters in the imagined situation. It is not so much that one chooses a subject, as that *it* chooses *one*. I was bowled over recently when a letter from Willa Cather came by a happy chance into my possession; in it she states categorically that she never wrote anything that did not come out of a direct and rather shattering personal experience.

Those cool and classic novels sprang from her blood.

Let me be specific: the idea for my novel *A Shower of Summer Days* came to me more than a year before I recognized it as a fertile idea for a novel. It came in the form of a small concrete incident or image. It happened that I was invited to stay for a few days at Elizabeth Bowen's old house in County Cork, Ireland, Bowen's Court. My room was a corner room, with four large windows; I remember Lowestoft bowls full of roses on small tables, silver candlesticks, a great red satin puff on the bed. But there was no desk. The first thing a writer does when he walks into a room is to look for a desk, and in a few minutes I had moved furniture around, taken a mirror, a bowl of roses, and the candlesticks off one of the tables, and pulled it over to the east window. I worked very happily there for days. But after I left, I found that I was troubled. Apparently in disturbing the ancient and noble order of a room in this great seventeenth century house, I had committed an outrage. An outrage upon what? "Custom and ceremony," Yeats might have answered; upon the beautiful form of a house which in itself had a strong personality. The seed of the novel was a psychic disturbance in me of an apparently negligible kind which began to *haunt*. Why was the house so powerful?

It soon became clear when the novel began to jell, that the theme would have to be the effect of a house on a group of characters. Conscious and unconscious began to work together. I can tell you now what at the moment of invention I could only sense, that if the house was to be the chief character in the drama, someone must be confronted by it who for one reason or another, felt antagonism toward the formal graces it embodied. Someone must come to the house at a crucial time in his or her life whom it could profoundly affect, even change. So Sally was born, an American girl in revolt against everything, shipped off to an aunt in Ireland to get over an unhappy love affair, a girl who arrives flaunting her blue jeans, and stumbles and falls on the great stone steps of the entrance.

If the house was to be a symbol of unchanging values, of a long continuity of ceremony and custom, then should not everyone in the novel be in a somewhat precarious state in relation to it? Why? Because the novel must dramatize its theme. If the house were taken for granted, there would be no dramatic confrontation. So Violet and Charles, the present owners, began to emerge in my imagination; they are victims of the dying British Empire and come back to the ancestral place as refugees from Burma at the time of the liberation. It is, thus, an early retirement for them, and a period of adjustment. I felt that there must be someone who represents the old ways, the continuity—so Annie, the cook, and Cammaert, the grumbling gardener forever complaining, forever remembering the great days when he was head gardener and had five men under him. Much later, when I had already written about a hundred pages, I came to the conclusion that the trio (Violet, Charles, and Sally) would have to become a quartet and so it did evolve with the importation of Sally's young man, Ian, from America.

But from the very beginning, for that was the seed of experience, the personal truth in this book for me, I knew that the *theme* would be the effect of a house on a group of people. I find only one long note about this novel in my notebooks. I then had in mind evidently only a short story. I jotted down about Sally, "sent to Ireland to get over an infatuation. But it was the last place not to remember in. The past flowed around everywhere like an air current. It assailed the nerves like a draft."

I think you must begin to sense through what I have been saying in such a rambling fashion, that theme and character determine plot. I have an idea that some beginning writers kill their novels by plotting too soon. Plot is, after all, only what has to happen because of cer-

tain characters set down in a certain situation. I would go
so far as to suggest that theme—the haunting question
the writer hopes to answer in the process of writing his
novel—*quickens;* plot—too early—*kills.*

So we have within us a quickening theme which has
magnetized characters around it. We may even have
written some tentative chapters letting the wind blow
where it listeth. But the time comes when the crucial
element is either there or not there: the novel must be
moving in a definite direction. One might suggest that
there is a bomb planted in the novel (the thing that happens). It may be simply a time bomb; the thing that
happens might conceivably be the passage of time, but it
is a bomb in the sense that when it explodes, the meaning
of the story becomes clear. All its diverse elements fall
into place and the grand design is visible to the reader.
Or, to change the metaphor, one might say that the novel
is a machine set in motion. It is moving toward a destination. What that destination is must be determined to a
large extent by theme. E. M. Forster has told us that
when he began *A Passage to India,* he knew that something important would happen in the Marabar Caves, and
that it would have a central place in the novel, but he did
not know at first what the "something" would be.

In my novel *Faithful Are the Wounds* the theme was,
perhaps, "Can a man be wrong and right at the same
time, wrong on one level and right on another and deeper
one?" If that is the question asked, obviously the novel
cannot move toward a complete justification of the main
character. In fact he commits suicide at the opening of the
book, and what interested me was not so much why he
did so, as what the effect of this violent act was on a group
of his friends and colleagues. The story moves toward an
epilogue some years after the suicide when those most
affected by it are under investigation by the McCarthy
Committee and the influence of their dead friend becomes
decisive.

This foreseeing of an eventual destination springs, I have suggested, from what one is trying to say, from the question asked. Practically it cannot be discovered until the writer has imagined the specific situation which will set the characters in motion. Theme, characters, and situation create plot. In Camus' *The Plague,* for instance, the characters are imprisoned in a city infected with plague. In William Golding's *Lord of the Flies,* the shipwrecked boys find themselves on an island, cut off from all contact with adults, and we watch the primitive forces of anarchy and violence take over the civilizing forces. In Virginia Woolf's *To the Lighthouse,* the situation is simply whether the weather will be fine enough for an annual family trip to a lighthouse. The trip is finally made, but not by the original group; some have died, all have been changed by time.

Of course the trouble with analysing a multiple process in this cold-blooded way is that one over-simplifies and above all, over-intellectualizes. Novels are not crossword puzzles. One can go back and discover *after* the event what probably made one decide this or that, but the fact is, of course, that one is literally dreaming up a novel, and dreams come from way below the conscious level. I remember with what delight I came, in Virginia Woolf's *A Writer's Diary,* on the first intimations of her greatest novel, *To the Lighthouse.* This is what she jotted down: "This is going to be fairly short; to have father's character done complete in it; and mother's; and St. Ives; and childhood; and all the usual things I try to put in—life, death, etc. But the centre is father's character, sitting in a boat, reciting 'We perished each alone,' while he crushes a dying mackerel."*

At the instant when that precise image dropped from her pen onto the page, she must have known that the embryo would live. What is splendid is that "etc.," for

*A *Writer's Diary.* Hogarth Press, London, 1953.

it is just that "etc.," a vision of life, which makes the book the great poem and critique that it is: "life, death, etc." Where to begin? You have characters, a theme, a situation; you know vaguely where the novel is going. But there is still the crucial question of point of view to be considered. Where is the camera eye? Is it to be way above in the sphere of omniscience, the writer as God who moves in and out of his characters at will? Is the whole drama to be witnessed by one central person, the camera? In a picaresque novel like *Don Quixote* or Saul Bellow's *Augie March* or *Huck Finn,* where the leading character is the thread who holds a series of episodes together, there is no choice. Obviously the book will be seen through the central character, whether it is written in the first or third person. In *Faithful Are the Wounds,* a concentric design, the central character alone is not seen from inside, for the point here is just his effect on a group of friends.

But one character, or possibly two, is always in high relief. The first big question is whether this main character is to be seen from inside or from outside? First novels can often be categorized as "What life does to Sam," and it is logical in this case to be inside Sam—*Of Human Bondage, Catcher in the Rye* are examples of this kind of novel. Life is usually hard on Sam and these novels are usually a criticism of society. The "I" has the ace in his hand, if the ace is the author's sense of values.

On the other hand, by limiting the view of life to one character, you do create problems for yourself, especially if the novel is written in the first person. Your "I" has to be on stage all the time, and there is little chance for the break in rhythm, the letting in of air, which descriptions of place and time, often make possible.

Possibly the danger of being inside one character alone is special pleading. Novels which present a general humanistic view, which do not "take sides," find the omniscient view, where the author steps in and out of his characters at will, more to the point. I am thinking, for instance, of Elizabeth Bowen, E. M. Forster, William Golding, Faulkner. On the other hand, the danger here is that there are no limitations. The novel may become uncentered, discursive, shapeless. The one-person point of view helps you shape a book. I had never tried it until my novel, *The Small Room*, but there the young teacher through whom the drama is witnessed is, primarily, an observer. I felt that this gave me a chance for irony—Lucy Winter is new on the academic scene. However, I might add that by the time the novel had achieved momentum, Lucy had become a participant: my talents are, I fear, not dispassionate.

Now at some point before you have begun to write, you will have a moment's vision of the whole book—a marvelous vision which you will not recapture until it is actually published—and often not then. You divine rather than know what it is to be, and this divining I, at least, look on as if I were seeing the whole meticulous effort ahead as a total painting. It composes itself: things are balanced against each other. The foreground and background figures take up their positions. There is a balancing of light and shade, of intensities relieved by moments of comedy or poetry, by a burst of sunlight from a window, or some quiet sheep in a field. Out of this seeing of the whole novel as if it were a painting, if you are lucky, you will feel a first scene emerging.

The first scene is radically important because here you set the mood, and hence the reader's state of mind, for the whole course. You are setting up a tempo. Is it to be a long intricate unfolding as in Proust? Then you can afford description, a slow building up of atmosphere, of time and place. Is it to be a book struck like a blow— Simenon, or Golding in *Lord of the Flies*—brief, economical, moving with implacable speed to a climax? Then you must set us down immediately in the center of a dramatic situation. The writer feels the imminent force of the book in his hands. He feels its potential speed.

Scene One establishes the rhythm of the book. My own *A Shower of Summer Days* begins with an easy-going description of the house. *Faithful Are the Wounds* begins with a wallop. The first evokes a long past of summers, suggests rain and sunlight, time, change, aspects of love, a romantic idyllic book. The other was designed to analyse the political anguish of our time in human terms, a complex, intense, driving book.

Scene One will introduce the major characters and place them in their way of life, together with a suggestion of the theme, of what the book is to be about. The major situation must be at least apprehended because this is what pulls the reader in. The first scene is, in fact, a spell. With it you win or lose—the novel while you are writing it, and eventually, the reader. Once the first scene is down it has set up a momentum which carries you, the writer, along willy-nilly. In this respect it resembles the first line in a poem. And sometimes, in the same way, comes out of the air, feels "inspired."

But if it feels inspired, it is because you have been half-consciously and half-unconsciously brooding this novel for months before a single word has been set down. You have been making shorthand notes to yourself; your characters have begun to talk to you in those hours between sleep and waking; and you have several times caught yourself saying to someone, "Yes, it's beginning to jell." This state is as exciting and uncomfortable as the stance of a diver on a high diving board just before he takes the dive. The first scene, even the first word set down is the terrifying moment when the "thing imagined" becomes reality. It is also a great relief.

Sometimes, intoxicated by swimming around at last, by being immersed in your material, the momentum of the first scene carries you along too fast; you lose sight of the whole vision which seemed so clear before you began to write; you forget that from now on, every word must be relevant to "the thing that is going to happen." The only rule of construction I know is to ask the question constantly, "Is this necessary?" Dialogue, for instance, cannot be used simply to focus or reveal character; it must carry the story forward. "Dialogue," Elizabeth Bowen has said, "is what the characters do to each other." And later on in the same enormously fertile "Notes on the Novel" she says, "It is to be remembered that *everything* put on record at all—an image, a word spoken, an interior movement of thought or feeling on the part of a character—is an event or happening."*

I myself think of a novel in process as a series of scenes. Each of these scenes is a miniature construction in itself, which must be prepared for, must then rise to a climax and, as it is solved, at the same time open a door into the next room or scene. But the scenes as they unfold are set on the curve of the whole book, a slowly rising wave which will break at the climax and resolve itself in the synthesis of the end. At the end of each chapter or section, some precipitation must take place between the characters, something must have changed. Of course some of this shaping is done when one has roughed out the whole thing and can revise for the dynamics of each scene in relation to the dynamics of the whole. I find myself cutting ruthlessly to keep the rising curve clean. It often happens that whole chunks can come out because what they convey is absorbed in the total drive of the book.

The design of a novel is an organic process. Because it is organic there is a danger in trying to formulate too precisely in a lecture such as this just what goes on. It is not possible, I am sure, to lay a whole novel out like a map; in the first place if that were possible, what would be the point of writing it? All the pleasure of exploration and discovery would be lost. For all the time you are writing, the novel is being constructed; it is constructing itself. The problem is to maintain creative fluidity and yet

*Collected Impressions. Alfred Knopf, New York, 1950.

hang on to the theme, the core of design, not to lose one's head, to keep feeling one's way and thinking one's way in close harness. The writing of a novel is a long sustained job, and one of the problems is that of holding so much in your mind, in balance, while you are actually at work on a tiny segment at a time.

"It all comes back," as Henry James says, "to the old, old lesson—that of the art of *reflexion.* When I practise it the whole field is lighted up."

Characters, if they are alive at all, prove to have an existence of their own, insist on breaking out of too arbitrary formulations. A character may change the whole tone of a novel by its intrusion, by its radical thrust up from the subconscious. This can be very disturbing, but it is surely a sign of life. . . ; the novel is beginning to exert its influence on its maker. When I began *Faithful Are the Wounds* I had intended to treat Isabel, the pro- tagonist's conservative sister, ironically. She was to incarnate the American middle-class woman, terrified of her radical brother (because he was so disturbing), clinging to the *status quo,* encased in a smug sense of superiority toward those conflicts which ended in suicide. But as I got inside Isabel, I found it impossible to maintain my ironic stance. The book itself was a desperate attempt to understand on the deepest human level the forces which, at the time of McCarthy, seemed to be about to tear this country apart. But you cannot understand any- thing until you are able to get inside it. Inside Isabel, I was forced to grow. Because of what Isabel taught me, I was able to make the book larger, saner, and actually more able to convince the Isabels of the world of what I had in my heart to say, than if she had been a contrived anti-hero. When James talks about the art of reflexion, this is what he means. It is a question of feeling, of sen- sitivity, of recognizing what is relevant *even when* it appears to be changing your design in a perilous way. It is also a matter of your relationship to your talent.

Are you able to grow with your book? Have you the courage to go back and re-write a hundred pages because of a change in emphasis? How far can you allow your characters to command you? I don't know how to answer that question, really, except perhaps by saying that they may be allowed to command you, as long as their own life forces you to deepen the direction of the novel, and not merely make for a rich digression.

In this brief essay we have actually covered perhaps two years' intermittent work. Telescoping time is one way of getting a bird's-eye view of the whole, but it can give no idea of the degree of anxiety, self-doubt, exhaustion, and sometimes even boredom which the writer himself goes through in the long process of writing his novel. There is always the danger of a failure of nerve. And this is the more true, the greater the body of work the writer carries along with him. It is easy to write a first novel; and the task of the novelist becomes increasingly difficult as one proceeds. Partly one knows more; what one is trying to say becomes more complex. Partly, anything achieved in the past becomes the enemy of the achievement of the present. Will it be as good as . . . is the dreadful question that lurks in the small hours of the night.

The stakes are high. In the last analysis they are certainly not fame, or money, but the stakes of life itself, that the writer be capable of indefinite growth. The writing of a novel is just as much of an experience in the very deepest sense as an actual experience, but it is an experience that you are fashioning into a work of art while you are having it. If you are not changed by your novel, if it does not teach you something you did not fully understand until you came to grips with it through setting your characters to work it out as if they really lived and you lived through them all, then there is small chance that it will magnetize readers to the troubling question it has asked.

Let us rest, at the end of the long, hopeful, intense struggle, on these words of Marcel Proust, who said of the novelist, "He must prepare his work minutely with perpetual regrouping of forces as for an offensive, must endure it like a fatigue, accept it like a Rule, construct it like a church, follow it like a regime, overcome it like an obstacle, conquer it like a friendship, nourish it like a child, create it like a world."*

---

*Le Temps Retrouve, II, 239-40 (translation, May Sarton).

The Writing of a Poem

SEVERAL DECADES ago Charles Abbott at the University library in Buffalo began asking poets for their work sheets and built up an extraordinary collection. Since then other libraries have followed suit and it is now possible for students in many parts of the country to explore a poet's mind at work, and to follow to its source what Marianne Moore has named "the feeling and precision, the humility, concentration and gusto" that must go into the writing of a poem.

But there is one thing that the work sheets on a single poem cannot show, and I must begin by speaking of it. I mean simply the state of being that precedes any writing. One might go so far as to say that the formal aspect of a poem, the craft aspect, is a game. The manipulation of certain words to make certain effects is a game not unlike a crossword puzzle or any other intellectual game with counters of one kind or another. What the work sheets show is the playing out of the game. What they cannot show is that, although poetry is a game, it is also a holy game; here, of course, it differs radically from the crossword puzzle. It is something more and something other than a purely intellectual amusement. In what does the "holiness" of the game of poetry consist? Is it not in the quality of the experience that precedes the writing? For the writing of poetry is first of all a way of life, and only secondarily a means of expression. It is a life discipline one might almost say, a discipline maintained in order to perfect the instrument of experiencing—the poet himself—so that he may learn to keep himself perfectly open and transparent, so that he may meet everything that comes his way with an innocent eye. How is he to achieve this extreme awareness and maintain it? Do you remember Thoreau saying, "To be awake is to be alive. I have never yet met a man who was quite awake. How could I have looked him in the face?"

No one could be asked to be "quite awake" all the time, but it is what the poet must ask himself more of the time than most people ask it of themselves. He must learn to induce a state of awareness. I use the word "induce" here quite deliberately. The mystic induces a state of extreme awareness, the visionary state, by certain disciplines, fasting, prayer, and so on. The poet must create his own disciplines. I myself have found that a good deal more solitude and a good many more empty hours than are usual in our "busy" civilization are one of my own requirements. I have to induce the state of awareness by renouncing some pleasures, the pleasures of society for instance. When I am writing I cannot afford to be out late at night. If I do go to a dinner party, I know that the next morning the edge will be a fraction less sharp, the edge of awareness. I shall not be "quite awake." What is inspiration, so-called, but the successful wooing of a state of mind?

And what is this state of mind? I can only speak for myself here. But for me it seems to be a floating suspension, above all the suspension of will: you cannot write a poem by wanting to write a poem, but only by becoming an instrument and that means not being knotted up to a purpose, but open to any accidental and fortuitous event. For this reasons trains and planes are very good places to lie in wait for poems. The telephone will not ring; and yet scenes float past, images well up; one can sit in a train and do nothing for hours without self-consciousness. So one autumn day I looked out of a train window at a tranquil bay, an absolutely flat pale blue ocean, and in the foreground a rowboat lifted very gently up on a long quiet wave. Just as we roared past I saw the wave break and ripple out on the lonely shore. The wave became for me the image of happiness, the shape of happiness. It became a poem. For what happens is that if the state of exceptional awareness is there, has been induced, this awareness will eventually collide with an object. The object may be something actually seen, seen with that peculiar intensity that acts like an explosion in the senses and through the mind, locking them together in a moment of "vision." Or it may be an incident, a feeling, an intuition that wells up from the subconscious without volition, sometimes taking the form of a single line.

So one might define the poem as the result of a collision between a state of awareness, a delicate instrument for registering sensation, and an object. For most of us, love is such an "object"; Paul Valery has gone so far as to say that "all poems are love poems." Conversely people in love become poets, if only for a few days or hours, because when one is in love one is "fully awake." I am sure you have had the experience of walking along a street and looking at every tree and bush as if it were a miracle, as if no one had ever seen such a wonder before as that patch of sunlight on that pavement—because you were in love!

This is the exact state of mind of the poet when he is ready to receive the poem. We are all aware that this state has in it an element of mystery. We can come right up to the edge of the mystery, but we cannot wholly define it. Let us allow a poet to speak of it, W. B. Yeats in fact, in a little poem that defines perhaps as well as anyone could "the holiness of the game."

> My fiftieth year had come and gone,
> I sat, a solitary man,
> In a crowded London shop,
> An open book and empty cup
> On the marble table-top.
>
> While on the street and shop I gazed
> My body of a sudden blazed,
> And twenty minutes more or less,
> It seemed, so great my happiness,
> That I was blessed and could bless.

Very young poets, you know, only wish to write about love. But as they grow older and more human, the range of experience which can excite them to the moment of inspiration widens, and this is one of the reasons why this art is such a great one. The demands it makes on intellect and the senses increase with age, and the excitement grows with age. We move, if we are worthy of our task, toward a purer innocence and a purer wisdom until at the very end we may attain what Coleridge has defined as the function of poetry, that state when the familiar is wonderful and the wonderful is familiar, and when the simplest object has seeds of revelation in it.

Simone Weil puts it, "Absolute attention is prayer." The eye of the poet must give to the object this kind of attention. He is to see what he sees as if it had been just created, and he is to communicate it to us as if we had never seen it before. But if you look at almost anything, a rock, a tree, a lizard in this way, you learn something. The prayer is in the looking; the answer to the prayer is the poem which describes the object and also does something more, is something more than the object itself.

Poetry one might say is the perpetual reincarnation of the spirit through a concrete image: "to see the world in a grain of sand."

We are now approaching the moment when the work-sheets begin. The poet is sitting on a train and has seen a wave rise and break on a lonely shore; he has had his moment of vision. He has felt deeply. He has been seized. He is in love, perhaps, or indignant, in a rage, more than usually excited. His state of mind is Miltonic:

> I have some naked words that rove about
> And loudly knock to have their passage out.

It is at this moment that something happens that forever divides the merely "poetic" person from the poet, the maker. For at this moment a transference takes place. What was high emotion is to be translated into a form, is to be "fashioned." And the process of this fashioning has nothing to do with whatever it was that set the poet off like a firecracker. That explosion is now over. The moment when the writing of a poem begins is a moment of high excitement, but of an entirely different kind to the experiencing of its birth as an idea for a poem. The moment the poet sits down to write, takes out his pad and doodles, his feeling which was essential, is no longer the point at all. He has had it. Unless it has happened to him already there will be no poem. What is important now is that this feeling be communicated to someone else by means of a created poem. The "poetic" person never makes this transition. He hugs his "feeling" to him and imagines it is a poem. The transference from experiencing to creating is in part a transference from feeling to thinking, a conscious exploration and manipulation of what the subconscious brings. This means that from now on in the shaping of his poem, the poet becomes a critic. He must be capable of unremitting ruthless analysis.

Too much has been said about metre and not enough

about what Jacques Maritain has called "the musical stir" that begins its rhythmic buzzing in the poet's mind. And Maritain goes on to speak of "a meaning set free in a motion." It is when one looks at metre from this point of view that its powerful magic becomes clear. For what the eventual definite metre in the poem must do is to awaken in the reader exactly the same sort of musical stir, and so *move* him. The musical stir, the form of the poem, is a spell.

What happens first? It has been my experience usually that a single line floats up into consciousness; is, if you will, "given":

"The memory of swans come back to you in sleep."

This line very often, not always, suggests the kind of musical stir the poem is to make, suggests the time, sometimes even the form.

It is just here that the amount of unconscious preparation the poet has been doing comes in. For now images must well up to be fashioned and these images will come from his subconscious mind. What has he been feeding it? What has he looked at, thought about, read, felt? Has he a passion for architecture? Has he been reading Traherne? Has he become lately fascinated by the Spenserian Stanza, or by a form such as the sestina? All this will be there now within his state of creative excitement. It is here that the general richness of the personality itself comes into play. In Robert Frost's case, for instance, all that real knowledge of the country world, the crafts of chopping wood, pruning trees, is there to provide images. The foreground of the poem is the specific emotion or sight or thought with which the poem is concerned. But the background is all that you are, have thought, felt, seen all your life. The subconscious will be very active at the moment you sit down and begin to doodle. Some of what it brings you will be incongruous, weak, or silly and it is here that the conscious mind goes to work, selecting, sharpening, slowly coming to formulate as exactly as possible what the musical stir only suggested. The creative process is a continual alternation between what is given and what is made of the gift.

I believe that if one were to isolate one quality and one only as essential to the poetic nature, it would be the poet's instinctive tendency to translate the abstract into the concrete, *to think in images.* For the business of poetry is to bring thought alive, to make a thought into an experience, and we experience through the senses. The means of doing this is the image.

So the experienced craftsman knows that he does not have a poem until one of these images brought to him by the subconscious hits him as true, as *the* communicative image. It is going to be his chief means of translating his feeling to a reader.

We are now approaching the moment when the beginner or the merely "poetic" person, in love with his own feelings, gives up. He has found a good image; the thing sounds roughly as he wants it to, and now he is stuck; he is lazy. And he has forgotten that although he may have had a wonderful feeling, no one else has had it yet. At this point the poet begins a four-hour or more stretch of intense analytic work, revising and revising; a tennis game is nothing to the actual effort required in the writing of a poem, the intensity of the effort. Worksheets will show that a finished poem may have gone through forty, fifty or more drafts before it emerges whole and clear and itself. For this is after all a complex object, this poem. It must convey a whole experience and must convey it musically and by means of images. The poet may, for instance, solve the problem of what form it will take, the metre and the rhyme-scheme, but battle for hours with one line that he cannot straighten out. He may have wonderful images, but be unable to find the tone, the music. Or he may spend one hour looking for one single verb.

For a long time the battle is drawn. Every poet has the experience of struggling for several hours, breaking down and re-building, and then having to admit that the whole thing is a botch. He has focussed it too soon, has tried to force it into the wrong rhythm, has not recognized certain signs that told him "that's the line to work from," and has chosen another, fruitless one. He may have thrown the gold away and kept the dross. Every one of us has had this experience because the risk is very great.

The creative process (and is this not also true of the educational process at its most creative?) is a breaking-down process as well as a building-up process. You may have to break your poem to remake it. The beginner hugs his infant poem to him and does not want it to grow up. He cannot stand the destructiveness implied in growth. And very often he is unwilling to allow his intellectual equipment to work in harness with his emotional and sensual equipment. But, says Mr. Yeats, "Love is created and preserved by intellectual analysis." Only the sentimentalist—at the opposite pole from the ruthless poet—refuses to acknowledge this fact:

> The stone resists: the chisel does destroy.
> But out of deprivation the grave image
> Slowly emerges and the sculptor's joy
> Is made out of a self-denying rage —
> Cut down and cast away, break to the core.
> Whatever easy triumph falls in chips
> And lies dispersed in waste upon the floor
> He gladly yields for the sake of those lips,
> That savage throat that opens the whole chest,
> Tension so great between him and the stone,
> It seems he carries vengeance in his wrist.
> Now take the chisel and make for the bone!
> Difficult love, you are the sculptor here,
> The image you must wrest, great and severe. *

---

*From *The Land of Silence*, by May Sarton, Rinehart and Company, New York, 1953.

Let us now see what the worksheets on a couple of poems might yield the student, and follow the process I have talked around at such length, quite simply, step by step. I do not apologize for using my own work here, because it is the only work where I know absolutely what the process was.

There is a poem called "Truth" in *The Land of Silence.* This poem came out of a difficult experience, a rather common human experience perhaps, but one that strikes each of us hard when we first have to face it. It is the experience of what gossip can do, and how one's own words or actions may be misinterpreted when they are carelessly bandied about. I have spoken of poetry as a discipline. I believe that the greatest discipline is that before one can write about an experience in a poem one must have understood it, or rather that before the poem is written, one will have come to understand it. One must have completely possessed and in some sense surpassed the occasion. The poem itself is a journey or discovery and self-analysis where self-pity or sentimentality can have no place. My own experience with gossip led me to examine what truth as far as human relations go may be, and how differently different human beings look at the same action. It was several months later before I had sufficiently assimilated this experience to be ready to communicate my findings.

The worksheets show first a note, "The human truth is no crystal but a prism." Beside this note I have noted possible rhymes for "prism": "chasm," "schism," "spasm," etc. Pretty depressing, you will agree.

There follow a series of phrases, separate short lines, suggesting that the musical stir here, the rhythm of the idea, required a short rather than a long line. I must have sensed that this idea of truth as a prism would best be communicated in a compact form, a form that might even suggest the shape of a prism on the page. The notes are quite prosaic:

> Is not mathematical
> You cannot say
> Of a person. He is this
> Once and for all.
> And the necessity to weigh
> The facets
> The strange new light
> Should induce tolerance
> Patience
> The virtues we exercise
> In training any dog.
> But forget in dealing
> With the human creature.

Very far from poetry still, as you can see! I then find:

> No one can tell
> Of another being
> This is the truth
> That I am seeing.

A rhythm is taking form, but these lines are bad, super-ficial, weighted too lightly for the weight of the idea. It's a jig. So I try again:

> Is no crystal
> But rather prism
> Catching many lights
> Turn it round and the view may change
> The facets are many.

(There's that word "facet" again.) There are pages and pages more of this battle to find the right words, the right form. Probably most of you, plagued by such notes, would have decided to give up. But I was stubborn; I was interested; and finally I did manage to fashion the poem "Truth" out of all these fumbles:

                    Truth
          Not visible
          After all
          Through a glass table,
          Air, or crystal
          Of open window,
          Transparent door,
          But less, or more —
          A prism maybe,
          Now blue, now green,
          And what you see
          I have not seen.
          For change the eye
          And what was true
          Becomes a lie:
          My green, your blue.
          For who can tell
          Just what was said?
          None hears it all:
          Your blue, my red.
          The human truth
          Is hard to sift,
          Alack, forsooth,
          Is apt to shift.
          Facet by facet,
          Ever vicarious,
          Definite, tacit,
          The light is various.
          My truth, your lie,
          My lie, your truth.
          See eye to eye?
          Alack — forsooth — *

(I have still got to find a way out of "alack, forsooth" one of these days.) I had not only achieved a passable poem by the long struggle, but I had also come to make peace with the experience. For poetry is, I believe, always an act of the spirit. The poem teaches us something while we make it. The poem makes you as you make the poem, and your making of the poem requires all your capacities of

---

*The Land of Silence, Rinehart and Company, New York, 1953.

thought, feeling, analysis, and synthesis. I hope this may suggest that there is nothing dull about revision.

As Stephen Spender has said in his very illuminating essay on "The Making of a Poem,"

> A poet may be divinely gifted with a lucid and intense and purposive intellect; he may be clumsy and slow; that does not matter, what matters is integrity of purpose and the ability to maintain the purpose without losing oneself. Myself, I am scarcely capable of immediate concentration in poetry. My mind is not clear, my will is weak, I suffer from an excess of ideas and a weak sense of form. *

Spender's modesty is consoling, for we know that he has achieved memorable poems, and he has done this partly at least because he has been able to discipline himself to prolonged and sustained revision. The problem of course is to keep one's excitement, not to lose the zest in the process. For as Spender proves so beautifully in his own work, "the result," so he tells us, "must be the fullest development in a created aesthetic form of an original moment of insight."

Sometimes one may even manage to rescue what seemed like a hopeless beginning. Sometimes an idea for a poem must tease the mind for years before it is ripe. And there are themes that must go on being explored as long as one lives. One of these is surely time. May I share with you one more set of my own worksheets, one of my struggles with this immense theme?

The poem is called "On Being Given Time." The occasion was my being given a Guggenheim Fellowship and for the first time in some years able to foresee an open space; I might at last hope to induce the state of peculiar awareness from which poems spring. I had finished a long and difficult novel; I was feeling tired and empty; and with this great news of imminent freedom in my pocket, I went for a walk. It happened that I came to

*The Making of a Poem, Hamish Hamilton Ltd., London, 1955.

one of the small ponds along The Fenway in Boston and stood for some moments watching the ducks swim about, watched, and suddenly experienced one of those "moments of vision" of which I spoke earlier. It is hard to define just what this moment contained; the work sheets we shall look at will gradually define it. At any rate I was seized by some intimation about time and what it is, and some weeks later the idea teased me into sitting down to try to capture it.

The first sheet is very much crossed-out, as well as written over along the margins. But I see I have circled a title: "Time as Creation." This evidently was the theme. I did not begin to write the poem until some weeks after watching the ducks, and in the interval I had evidently forgotten the original key to the experience. The early work sheets are really hunting expeditions in pursuit of an image. There are three separate tries; each of them shows the signs of battle:

The first reads:

> Time is the joker in every pack
> A mechanical toy that life winds up
> The magician who makes time disappear
> The necromancer
> The gangster, the shady thief —

One can see clearly in the lines that poets work by association just as the analysand does within a psychoanalytic analysis. The second try goes off on a different track. There are two or three versions of this one:

> I stalked it all day among the pigeons
> The automobiles, the jet-planes, faster, faster,
> Laid in wait for it at street corners
> Spreading my nets of silence over the noisy regions
> As if to catch a cloud and make time fall like rain
> But at the end the joke was on me

As, yes, the target of the day hunted the hunter

Hit by my own target at the end

But although this evidently had possibilities, since I gave it three tries, I was still not in the groove. So there is a third:

Children know better than to take it
Playing the long game of morning large and free

Animals rest within it and never let it —

(I might interpolate here that these lines were finally the focussing ones for the poem, but I did not recognize this yet. I went off on another tangent):

Only do *we* make this mechanical toy
Count it like money as if so large and free
It could be hoarded and amassed.
It cannot ever be spent.

We can be part of its flowing and so spend ourselves
But spend time? Take time? Give it away?

This last seemed for awhile to be *it,* and after playing around with three or four versions based on the suggestion of the last line above, I came out with what looked like a poem, and titled it,

Journey Toward Time

They say "it takes time"
Or "take your time," they say.
Mine? My time? My lifetime?
And how do you "take it" anyway?

Once I clenched my fist
And snuffed time like a moth;
I learned there's more of a twist
To catching it than truth.

They say, "Time's money," too,
But could you count it piece by piece
Hoard or keep the river's flow?
Invested, would it still increase?

"Tell me the time." Who can?
Watches are time's worst enemy;
The little tick is fatal.
It's not mechanical at all.

Oh it's no friend to men
The winged chariot or jet-plane
That screams him round and round the sun
Until his heart bursts and he's done.

Yet I've come close to seeing
The angel out of the corner of an eye —

There I left it. Why? Because I sensed just about here that what I was doing was writing *about* the subject; I was playing with words, instead of translating the experience. The tone of voice also was not quite my own. It seemed a little slick, too light. What I really wanted to do was to make the reader actually feel time opening out while he read, not to tell him what had happened to me or how I felt about it, but to communicate the experience itself. I remember I gave up at the end of that day. And waited for several days, with the poem knocking around in the back of my mind, while I did other things.

Then I picked up the crossed over, re-written, mess of worksheets and studied them. I found that the first one seemed the most alive; I re-read it in its various versions and found a note I had overlooked:

The ripple behind the duck as it swims
The release after music

This was clearly the kind of image I was looking for, the image that made the thing happen instead of just talking about it. There then began the search for the stanza form:

> We may be sick of time, but time's the healer,
> Angry with time, but time's the peace-giver
> Afraid of time, but time —
> Destroyed by time, but time is also saviour

But this was obviously playing with words again, allowing the rhyme to distort the idea. However, I was getting warm, and a few pages further on I find this:

> There might be some device worth discussing
> The ripple behind the duck as it swims
> Opening the way to time without fussing
> Or that other ripple after music that breaks down walls.
> I have taken a walk round the block in the evening
> After the crowded day, renewed acquaintance
> With time as the most natural thing.
> I have seen it floating through a dance.

Here is the first appearance of what turned out to be crucial in the final poem, the idea that form releases the sense of time. I hope that under all these words that cannot come close to the complex of feelings, thoughts, analysis that go into the hours of working at a poem—I hope that under the words you have sensed that I was all the time clarifying my idea. The search for the image was part of that clarification. I only knew, you see, what the experience had really contained when I had discovered the true image for it. When this happened I had the form, a rather slow-moving rhythm, a five-line stanza. For as Emerson puts it so beautifully:

> It is not metre but a metre-making argument that makes a poem, a thought so passionate and alive that like the spirit of a plant or animal, it has an architecture of its own.

Just as the poem makes the poet, so the idea also creates its own form.

I was now well on my way. At the end of another five or six hours I had the poem. Here it is in the version of that time:

On Being Given Time

Sometimes it seems to be the inmost land
All children still inhabit when alone.
They play the game of morning without end,
And only lunch can bring them, startled, home
Bearing in triumph a small speckled stone.

Animals, too, live in that open world.
We may tease up the sleeping furry ball,
But starfish paws will gently be unfurled
And furled again, and the cat all recurled
So roundly, the interruption quite unreal.

Scholars and lovers make the midnight blaze,
Spring an hour open to hold three centuries.
They are the joyful jugglers of the days,
Replacing clocks, those rigid enemies,
With thought and passion conjured as they please.

We have been long aware that time's no toy
To be manipulated like a clever engine
With little hands that tick away all joy.
Sweet flowing time the children still enjoy
Has natural and nonchalant dimension.

Yet even for them, too much dispersal scatters;
What complex form the simplest game may hold!
And all we know of time that really matters
We've learned from moving clouds and waters
Where we see form and motion lightly meld.

Not the fixed rigid object, clock or mind,
But the long ripple that opens out beyond
The duck as he swims down the tranquil pond,
Or when a wandering falling leaf may find
And follow the formal downpath of the wind.

It is, perhaps, our most complex creation,
A lovely skill we spend a lifetime learning,
Something between the world of pure sensation
And the world of pure thought, a new relation,
As if we held in balance the globe turning.

Even a year's not long, yet moments are.
This moment, yours and mine, and always given,
When the leaf falls, the ripple opens far,
And we go where all animals and children are,
The world is open. Love can breathe again.

Yes, there does come the moment, the wonderful moment when the poem is finished, when you have rolled a page into the typewriter for the last time and are ready to send it out to friends. There is nothing more you can do. It is on its own. This, of course, is the moment when it is quite necessary to try it out on someone, preferably at once, for already in a few hours the "first fine careless rapture" of achievement will be attacked by doubts, and the revulsion that may have something to do with fatigue will begin to creep in. W. B. Yeats in a letter to a friend comments:

> One goes on year after year gradually getting the disorder of one's mind in order, and this is the real impulse to create. Till one has expressed a thing it is like an untidy, unswept, undusted corner of a room. When it is expressed one feels cleaner, and more elegant, as it were, but less profound, so I suppose something is lost in the expression: *

Is that the end? Not quite. Much later on I had a letter from Archibald MacLeish suggesting that the poem would benefit by some cutting. He suggested cutting everything except stanza four and the last three. Well, I thought about this for three years, and played around with various cuts, and finally put the poem into my book, *In Time Like Air*, with five stanzas, cutting two, three and four of the version quoted earlier in this essay.

I cannot imagine whether in all I have said there has been some small part of the "usable truth" for you. Perhaps, if nothing else has emerged, at least the idea that inspiration is facile, or that poems spring like Athene

---

The Letters of W. B. Yeats, Macmillan and Company, New York, 1955.

fully-armed from the poet's brow has been exploded!
But surely whatever I have failed to communicate, I
trust that I have not failed to communicate my faith that
poetry is a way of life as well as a complex and fascinating
intellectual game, that poets must serve it as a good
servant serves his master, must revere and woo it as
the mystic reveres and woos God through self-discipline
toward joy. And I hope that you may feel under all these
words the inexhaustible enthusiasm that drives us on,
that willingness to break down in order to refashion closer
to the heart's desire that makes the creative process
among the most fruitful and awe-inspiring disciplines
of the mind.

Revision as Creation

MY THESIS is that revision *is* creation and that it is a far more exciting and revelatory process than the mere manipulating of word and idea, though at its lowest level it is, of course, also that. My thesis is that we *earn* form as we earn understanding; my thesis is that metaphor ("to see the world in a grain of sand") is the great teacher of the poet as he wrestles to discover what he really means, just as it is the point for the reader where intellect and emotion fuse and he meets the poem as he might meet a person with whom he is to fall in love at first sight. But this impact, the impact of a true poem, must have been preceded by a long adventure on the part of its creator: for him what is the value of the finished work compared to what he has found out on the journey of its making?

I understand very well why Valery simply could not bear to "finish" a poem; what interested him was revising it—indefinitely—because he was discovering so much on the way; because he felt that a moment of inspiration could be, in fact, mined forever. It was the same attitude that Yeats expressed in four lines:

> The friends that have it I do wrong
> Whenever I remake a song
> Should know what issue is at stake:
> It is myself that I remake.

For me a true poem is on the way when I begin to be haunted, when it seems as if I were being asked an inescapable question by an angel with whom I must wrestle to get at the answer. We all experience at times the pressure of the unresolved crude matter that we need to set outside ourselves and to examine; the poet's way of doing it is to begin to make some notes, to ease the tension by writing something down on a pad and looking at it. At this point it is often not at all clear what the poem is really about. At this point what goes down on the page may be quite incoherent, *because* whatever has been set in motion is complex . . . and because it has probably come out of a strong emotion, but one that is, for one reason or another, troubling. One thing is sure: somewhere among the jottings there will be an image, because it is the nature of poetry to turn the abstract into the concrete. Very possibly there are several images and I begin to know what the poem is telling me as I probe them, turn them over like pebbles picked up on a beach, hold them in my hands, feel their substance and weight, dream them alive in my mind. "Here we are at a place," says Gaston Bachelard* who has taught us so much about the psychology of image-making, "where ideas dream and where images meditate."

The image must be complex enough to carry the weight of complex feeling; it must be absolutely exact. This is where the beginner often bogs down; he is too easily satisfied with the flotsam and jetsam the wave of what

---

*See especially *L'Air et Les Songes* (Paris: Corti, 1943) and *L'Eau et Les Reves* (Paris: Corti, 1942).

might be called inspiration has brought him. He is unwilling to analyze, to probe, to push the limits on what seems to him marvelous, unexpected, and a gift from the gods. Beginners are narcissistic and conservative; it takes time to learn to be daring and radical enough to break down again and again, and by doing so to explore the most elusive realities of experience in the most concrete and exact possible terms.

It has happened to me at least once that the image preceded the poem by years. I tucked it away for the moment when it would meet the experience worthy of it for intensity and complexity. Such an image was suggested to me by that same Bachelard: "Salt dissolves and crystallizes; it is a Janus material. To dream salt intimately is to penetrate into the most secret habitation of one's own substance." When I first came upon that image I knew I was not ready to use it but that someday I would be. The poem, a love poem, which finally got built on that image is itself an example of how one tests a metaphor. If you like, the whole poem analyzes the image to prove something about the nature of love in relation to time.

In Time Like Air

Consider the mysterious salt:
In water it must disappear.
It has no self. It knows no fault.
Not even sight may apprehend it.
No one may gather it or spend it.
It is dissolved and everywhere.

But, out of water into air
It must resolve into a presence,
Precise and tangible and here.
Faultlessly pure, faultlessly white,
It crystallizes in our sight
And has defined itself to essence.

What element dissolves the soul
So it may be both found and lost,
In what suspended as a whole?
What is the element so blest
That there identity can rest
As salt in the clear water cast?

Love, in its early transformation,
And only love, may so design it
That the self flows in pure sensation,
Is all dissolved and found at last
Without a future or a past,
And a whole life suspended in it.

The faultless crystal of detachment
Comes after, cannot be created
Without the first intense attachment.
Even the saints achieve this slowly;
For us, more human and less holy,
In time like air is essence stated.

—*Cloud, Stone, Sun, Vine*
(New York: Norton, 1961)

Perhaps you can imagine what a long struggle it was to get inside this metaphor and through it to discover what I was trying to say about love! "What do you go into a poem for?" asks Robert Frost. "To see if you can get out!"

It is hard to talk about revision because it is a complex matter. One of the ways one is helped to "get out" what is "in" the poem, is form. The poem I have just read is exceedingly compressed; the form itself creates intensity. You can't wallow—you have to *control*. I have said that form is earned. What I mean by that is that the music of a poem does not show itself unless one's whole being is at a high pitch of concentration. The experience back of the poem must have been revelatory. The trouble with free verse is that very rarely (D. H. Lawrence comes to mind as an exception) does the intensity seem great enough; the danger is the diffuse, self-indulgent, not closely enough examined content.

If the pressure back of the poem is great enough, then I find almost always that among those rough chaotic notes I jot down in the moment of inspiration, there is one line that suggests meter, and sometimes I can sense the whole first stanza. It is here in the music of the poem that the greatest mystery lies. I suppose that a practising poet has inside him the rumor of many sounds, the patterns of poems by others which he has totally absorbed. He doesn't say—ever—that he is going to write a sonnet; he has a sonnet idea; a sonnet hums inside this idea, and the form is inevitable if it is to be valid. We do not impose form on the poem; form is organic. But just as with the image, the poet in a state of inspiration may go wrong unless he is extremely self-critical. The enemies of creation are and have always been facility, cleverness, self-indulgence, and above all a misunderstanding about what inspiration is. I know that I am inspired when I become a fury of self-criticism to dig out what I really mean from a lot of irrelevancies that have poured down on the page in the first excitement of the start.

Revising a poem means being possessed by a driving need to clarify a powerful and complex experience by means of image and form. When one is well into it and maybe ten or twelve pages of the struggle are already strewn about, it is clear that the feeling which drove one to make the struggle for expression is no longer the point. Something else has taken its place, which I must call the act of *creation*, and the act of creation implies a conscious exploration and manipulation of what the subconscious brings. The poet has become a critic. He must be capable from now on in of unremitting ruthless analysis.

Sometimes one has to wait a long time before one can sense the form. "It is not meter," says Emerson, "but a meter-making argument that makes a poem, a thought so passionate and alive that like the spirit of a plant or animal, it has an architecture of its own." Some poems are inward gestations; they haunt; they bother; they work their way through a long inward process of refinement. During the time when the Nazi camps were being uncovered I needed to speak about it (we all felt the crushing weight of horror and had to come to terms with it somehow). I had the image—it was that of a gentle cousin of mine in Belgium, the weakling of the family who had never made much of himself, but who, when the supreme test came of withstanding torture and not telling, found it in him to die rather than to speak. Now here was an example of an emotion at first too strong to do anything with; I just had to live with it for a long time, to come through it into some usable truth. It had to be completely *faced* first with a cold honest look. Revision is creation because we are making ourselves through the making of the poem. There are no notes. A poem is not a scream and good poems are never hysterical, so the scream must have been inwardly suppressed before the poem, that which will communicate, and in this instance make the unbearable bearable, can find its way out. One of the ways in which poetry does what Rilke asks of it ("you must change your life") is because of its *music*. But I could not find the music for a long time, because I had not resolved the emotion. Perhaps you can imagine the relief when I was able to write what turned out to be a ballad, a rather simple song. I hope it does not run away from the reality, but transforms it into usable truth.

The Tortured

Cried Innocence, "Mother, my thumbs, my thumbs!
The pain will make me wild."
And Wisdom answered, "Your brother-man
Is suffering, my child."

Screamed Innocence, "Mother, my eyes, my eyes!
Someone is blinding me."
And Wisdom answered, "Those are your brother's eyes,
The blinded one is he."

Cried Innocence, "Mother, my heart, my heart!
It bursts with agony."
And Wisdom answered, "That is your brother's heart
Breaking upon a tree."

Screamed Innocence, "Mother, I want to die.
I cannot bear the pain."
And Wisdom answered, "They will not let him die.
They bring him back again."

Cried Innocence, "Mother, I cannot bear
It now. My flesh is wild!"
And Wisdom answered, "His agony is endless
For your sake, my child."

Then whispered Innocence, "Mother, forgive,
Forgive my sin, forgive—"
And Wisdom wept. "Now do you understand, Love,
How you must live?"

—Cloud, Stone, Sun, Vine

There was no problem with the image here, of course. It was given and it was archetypal. The problem was the music, was the *form.*

If we earn metaphor by being extremely open to experience of all kinds, and able to examine it with a cold clear eye, and if we earn form only as we are able to experience at a high level of intensity, then might one not say that the revising of a poem is a constant revising, disciplining and refining of the poet himself? Creation is revision within the whole person as he moves on from youth to middle age and from middle age to old age. Yeats is, of course, the great exemplar, for he molded his whole art when he was an old man. Each true poem has been an act of *growth*, and growth is not something that can be pasted on or arrived at by putting on a new dress or cutting one's hair in a new style. Let me suggest, then, that the art of poetry as a lifetime adventure will demand the capacity to break down over and over again what has already been created, and to break down barriers within the poet's self so that he may keep on growing within the whole form and shape of his life.

On Growth and Change

At Lindos

"What are ruins to us,
The broken stones?"
They made for the sea,
These elementals
Possessed by Poseidon.
"And what is Athene?"
The sun flamed around them.
The waters were clear green.

What compelled us
To face the harsh rock?
Why did we choose
The arduous stairways?
There lay the crescent
Of white sand below us,
And the lucky swimmers.

67

But at last we came out,
Stood high in the white light,
And we knew you, Athene,
Goddess of light and air,
In your roofless temple,
In your white and gold.
We were pierced with knowledge.
Lucidity burned us.
What was Poseidon now,
Or the lazy swimmers?
We looked on a flat sea
As blue as lapis.
We stood among pillars
In a soaring elation.

We ran down in triumph,
Down the jagged stairways
To brag to the bathers,
But they rose up to meet us
Mysterious strangers
With salt on their eyelids,
All stupid and shining.

So it is at Lindos,
A place of many gods.

> —*A Private Mythology*
> (New York, Norton, 1966)

I HAVE BELIEVED from the start that it would be possible to go on growing indefinitely as a poet, believed it against some of the evidence: Rimbaud, who ceased to write; Wordsworth who doddered on too long—though each had powerful genius. But there are stars we can hitch our wagons to, Yeats for one, who broke and re-made his style when he was in his forties and wrote some of his great poems in his seventies.

The poet in middle age must take risks at an age when this is harder than it was in youth, must learn how to remain open, "transparent" is my word for it, at a time in life when his friends in less demanding professions are consolidating gains and deepening the groove of hard-won personal style. Poetry is a dangerous profession because it demands a very delicate and exhausting balance between conflict and resolution, between feeling and thought, between becoming and being, between the ultra-personal and the universal—and these balances are shifting all the time. We move softly because we tread on swords; we move quietly to remain aware of the slightest stir in the grass, as well as of the plane breaking the sound barrier overhead; we move about without defense, totally open to experience whatever it may bring. The instinct to protect oneself is very strong; the poet cannot afford to allow this instinct to preserve him from growth. His mastery, I sometimes think, is chiefly the mastery of anguish and doubt.

I have chosen "At Lindos" as the thread on which to hang these observations for more than one reason. We need to rejoice in the fertility of poetry in the United States today. We too are nourished and renewed by many gods; we have poets of genius who range all the way from a traditionalist like Richard Wilbur to those new voices who are breaking the sound barrier in *their* way. It is this wide spectrum that makes poetry so rich and exciting; it is being read in a way that perhaps the novel has ceased to be—perhaps because it is alive in a way that the novel is no longer.

I have chosen "At Lindos" also for personal reasons. It was the breakthrough from formally structured verse into free verse, which I had not found appropriate to my uses for many years. Is this return to a more fluid, and elusive, style one of the demands of middle age, a time when the need is felt for a less strained breathing, for a larger dimension? I have believed that intensity commands form. The poem I was writing seemed ex-plosive and vital in proportion to the tension it could

support, and that tension presupposed formal struc-
turing. When I was in a state of intense perception,
lines ran through my head and would have their way, and
taught me, as I put an average lyric through thirty to
sixty drafts, where the poem meant to go and how it
would get there.

Formal structure satisfied the need for the absolute.
After those thirty drafts had been worked through, I
could sometimes feel, "There, it's finished. All is held
solid and clear and contained; there is nothing ragged or
spilled over. I can hold it in my hand like a rock."

Yet my book *A Private Mythology* is about half in
free verse. We have seen the same phenomenon in
our great poet Robert Lowell, who moved from the
explosive intensity and formal structure of his early
poems to a much freer style in his last years.

It took me three years of abortive attempts at putting
the essence of a first visit to Japan, India, and Greece,
into formal verse, before I could admit that I was on the
wrong path. The poems felt over-manipulated, and died.
I had embarked on that great adventure to celebrate
my fiftieth birthday, and I sensed that this was to be a
time of painful transition.

Finally, after three years, I took a deep breath and
plunged into a new element. . . ; it was all risk and tremor
at first. I had to break down a grooved response to meter;
iambic pentameter had become my natural way to write
poems. This fluid element of free verse was frightening.
I found that its value for the reader of apparent spon-
taneity, casualness, was just as hard to come by as the
sustained dancing quality of formal structure. In the first
place, in free verse the alternatives are almost without
limit, and so the temptation to revise indefinitely is always there. I found it hard to bring the poem out to the
sense of finality I had grown accustomed to, the joy of
achievement. These poems felt not like rocks in my hand,

but like water flowing over it. Free verse is far closer to normal breathing. I missed the tension between the speaking voice and the strict form of which Robert Frost has spoken so eloquently.

But little by little I learned to breathe with the line; I enjoyed the sensation of being floated on an image, on a sentence to its very end. The free verse poem, I discovered, runs on unbroken. It achieves momentum, and rounds itself out chiefly by means of metaphor. Where the poem in meter dances, the free form saunters, stopping here and there, as a walker does. The silences within it are, perhaps, even more important than those within metrical form, but they are achieved by more subtle means. In "At Lindos" every break between the lines should create a space in the mind, should simulate the passage of time, a pause.

Because free verse approaches the conversational, every device which can make it immediate is to the point. In "At Lindos" one of the problems I had to solve was to explain the setting, and to set up a dialogue, and I hope that the opening question does just this. But of course the conversation in a poem is as stylized as it is in any work of art, as stylized as the dialogue in a Hemingway short story.

The greatest peril in free verse seems to be that of over-charging, or of rambling along, so that cutting to the bone becomes mandatory. It must feel shaped, though in a far less obvious way than in a sonnet, for instance. And I fear, even now, after being subjugated by the adventure, that no free verse poem is as *memorable* as a poem in form may be. It exists more like a light-bird on the ceiling than like a rock. It is always in flight. It does not, perhaps, give rest. But what it can give the reader as well as the writer is a sensation of things opening out, a horizon, not a boundary. It has its own way of disturbing.

For poetry exists to break through to below the level of reason where the angels and monsters that the amenities keep in the cellar may come out to dance, to rove and roar, growling and singing, to bring life back to the enclosed rooms where too often we are only "living and partly living."

Text set on Compugraphic Execuwriter II in 12 point English,
quotations in 10 point.
Titles and cover set on StripPrinter in Palatino semi-bold.
Photocomposition and page makeup by Merle Hillman.